NEW LIFE

JoAnna Novak

www.blacklawrence.com

Executive Editor: Diane Goettel
Cover Design: Zoe Norvell
Cover Art: "Dawning" by Max Gottlieb
Book Design: Amy Freels

Published 2021 by Black Lawrence Press.
Printed in the United States.

Contents

IV.

V.

to N–

Will you glimmer on the sea?
—H.D., "Moonrise"

I

*

What in the straining body can be immobilized?
—Roland Barthes, *A Lover's Discourse*

Progress

You are as long as a gerbil, toilet paper tube, cassette tape, harmless bit
    of pipe—
I file you away, my scarlet clue. Half an ear on ice then nose to powder,
I vitamin in the garden underneath the peacock umbrella.

And brochures call this power?

I was asleep at the table, dreaming of a foil swan, chewing
a napkin or a Buddha's hand, I didn't care, anything would do.

Free food all over. And more when everything's a measure:
sleeve of crackers, packet of peanut butter—
in the conservatory, in the dining room, study, the lobby.

Big as a butternut, round as a watermelon, you are so hungry
you swallow the revolver, the wrench, the room key

and me, my whole life.

New life

does not survive on protein alone. My ankles are bound
to tear marching this reef, yet what a thrill—bloodying
white pumps. The island is mine. A mole on earth's back,
bull's eye, bingo, scratch, bite. At seven and twelve and thirteen
weeks, the pulse shimmers like a firefly: interruption.

Suddenly the weight is bready, tedious. Hammocks tilt,
Zombies spoil the lagoon. I shouldn't take such immoderate
companions for granted, but it's hot and the clams are bad
in the shallows. Tiring of fish and tea, dreaming of chips
and beer, I am told: Pack a suitcase. Keep near an open line.

The island is round and lovely green
from the perimeter massy buggy rotten
marshy sore-breeding vomitory delusion-
invoking Stockholm syndromic desperation
forty feet from shore—adorable, ordeal, ordure.
A crow helicopters hopes of rescue. I wave
the arms I have. I do not need civilization
nor another Fiji. Triple prison, please. Inter-
coastal. Tied to a shock. Tethered to stones.
Beaten by waves. Buffeted into orgasm.

I need shipwreck ribs to get off. Privacy done as coconut fluff.
I wish for garters, typing paper, pompom earrings, ice, rubber,
raspberries, raffia cord, black bikinis, the augury of fingers
and wrists in a room where I can loosen from myself,
a vacancy that means ...

The Hungry

Some hide their suffering behind black glasses. Others try
new haircuts. On the lawn they hear a gospel of sons preached
by a man in shorts. I do not join the picnic. I spend my days on
the balcony, watch the syncretists in the courtyard, look out
over the water at the rock. In the distance, it collects moss and
barnacles. Why do I call the rock a rock? The rock is a
mountain, hard, intrusive, protruding on the horizon.

Now, the sky dark. The lawn emptied—most have left, full
and moist. The rock gone with the sun, sun sunk in caldera, if
I cannot see it, I cannot sleep. The rock disinvites lying on my
back, my side. I dream on foot, leaving the room as a vapor. To
stand, to swim, to boat to it, coat it in wishes and footprints: is
that too much to beg for confinement?

(Here comes a husband, beer strapped to his back—some
kindness.)

Morning, the rock is breakfast under a dome: Mont Blanc.
Along the balcony, I roll the empty stroller. I can be honest
with the child. I hate its topography, but I like to watch the
rock. The rock invites teens, wine, lilac skies, cummy
tummies, tiki life, sloshed life, lost life until the stars show up
the sun and I'm back to eavesdropping gospels. Hollow rock,
bladder bloat: swollen balloon in reeds. Me spelling rearview
sermons, cursing the cost of vacation.

Trimester

Venomous, the arm shows red and assertive,
        sensate all along. Harder to spear the insula

              or shore this dark brain,
    the manifest throbbing—pulse

      is perfect, blood pressure cuffed,
        even these veins are good—
            succulent, fat
    (python in reeds, pining for a kill).
Little flinching. The paper skirt over me
                  stays dry and still.

      But here, let's have some light,

little boy (our checkup tests fluorescents).

           The doctor stands and pretends
      to come through the door once more,
          urges my uterus under the paper
              (piss-sopper, jelly-wipe, quilted, pink).

     You've got it pretty bad, he spills,
          pills from the keyboard, pills swivel-click,

           purse bugs,
           water bugs,
           Hydroxycut,
           minus a line in my palm.

**

He works his wedding band frown,
            tells me
    No one would be better off without you.
      (Just lie down.)

      Pill prayer, pill prize, the exemplars are so familiar, mouse down
         the gulch, hatchery jaw, jam it in, jam it now,
            deeper, harder, attagirl:

                      diabetes insulin
                      stress fracture rest
                      pens peanuts bees.

         He touches his arm. Imagine infected
flesh, rashy and hot.
              Truth or silent dare?
        (Just taste the word: *crutch.*)

You are a mom now, he says, wifemothermarm,
     mothball, mum, mutterer. From him,
         a wrinkled whitecoat? Give me grander

     reptiles on this inhospitable island. Garter on a swing tray,
        diamondback tub,
Animal, I don't want to go in   the pool
            and I won't lose my tongue

      and I won't like your table. Give me ether,
   at least twilit sleep, Tonga Room
         dreams, trek over stream,
            rain and rum on the half hour—

Stethoscope speaks: *You're a little too familiar*
with terms—ideation, ideation, passive

  ideation—well, damn you, diction,
thoughts, mots, motile woman,
  back to your continental shelf!

This is not the way things have to be.

  Your mouth might stay.
  Your face will freeze. When your eyes cross,
you'll regret that Mother Hubbard you don like a saint.
  You'll never be free again (poor mussel in a sack).

  **

I have a hand; he shakes it.
  Elevator, garage, pack:
  my leave.

  Do you blight me, little boy?
  Reprieve this wet channel,
  our runaway atoll, baby
  island, sweet Terabithia of
  everything impossible?

  The antidote is encyclopedic:
  Isolation can be achieved in many ways, most often
  through some geographical context.

  This beach is dark and endless
  —not a problem.

N is for Nurture

No, don't
believe me;

I don't
believe me

either.
I was

the only
one

without
an

empty
stomach.

Cock: Anamnesis, 04.19.19

I wanted a private beach. He wanted to take me below the bank and let me open the safe. Cocking his head, the miracle man showed me his miry root. Ruckling. Spoiled. He wanted to crack my knuckles, puddle my ink, twist me by the pinky, fat me on roses, raze the islands in my fingerprints, blur the whorls.

Everything was lost when I took off my sunglasses, but the man insisted. Have a sonogram! His baize daybed, algal fountain. He likes me big and blind and behaving—at least until siesta. Then, I can waddle the grounds, see the poquitas, feed the nannies pineapple leather. All I have to do is keep my leash. Say I am leashed to his cock. Kissing it, bleeding, hurting for it: no, I don't faint. Finally, I get to the beach.

I saw it from a distance, a wing where earth meets sky. This morning, I'm sure, I saw it still. I face what I know is there. I don't say much anymore: our plane disappeared in the mountains.

Gaslight

Far away, closets open. Out come the towels. White coats the
walls.

Vidal, voila, this hair!

A clatter kitchens: liver in fry pan, yogurt-clot drain, coffin fridge,
spit.

Rattles, babbles, crochet clicks. Cheepy birds, peeky crabs,
gurgles.

What have you done to him?

Summoning props to rehearsal, minus moral dilemma, the weeks
went aimless, wandering.

What's in a crib?

Give it a paint. Oil the wheels. Mattress, counterpane.

Witchy.

Lose the drapes, let in Manhattan.

(Far away, the Hudson's plenitude: give thanks.)

—or, seventy-five times, raise and lower the shoulders, palms
together in prayer: *grant me freedom to mean more.*

Crazy girl, why would you watch that?

Alien strength

that evening, when I was moved   into a bigger room

with a bigger bed, still   not
wanting

to fold my hands, paper moth over motherhood,

with a man standing the corner, tearing brioche

from room service. Using noumena

soft as opals and sneaking about the proscenium,

where digestives stale and trebles cull
dust—

it's the only way

to be a normal person.

II

*

Each day her longing grew and because she knew she could not have it, she began to pine and look pale and miserable.
—Lore Segal, "Rapunzel"

Volatiles

As a young woman, my mother lost her hair when the oven
erupted. Eyebrows gone, eyelashes singed, her bangs frizzled
like La Choy. She screamed and screamed and, bent over the
capsular island in the kitchen, kept screaming. Here, I still
hear her: eruptive, unguarded, cursing her house.

The smell of curling iron and burnt peanuts.

Cereal on a sheet.

Yesterday, I asked what she was doing. This and that. What's
that? One thing or another. Zapping a patty, not broiling—
one less thing. Now her arches ache. And it bothers her,
missing out on my change, she feels really, really sorry for
herself. I twist my ponytail. I asked.

Cartography

The map thickens, reddens, doubles

—swarms with iron,   binds in vitals,
        I am more fluid than food.
            Some legend clangs from the gate.

                But at least there are cabbage-palms

and thinking like a baby means thinking like a bee.

In a trice, I try the key. See

      a galère of gardenia girls

                —how pretty you look with your belly!
                —is this your first?

crow's knot cording,

          numb pump

     of forward moves,

          my coordinates spoke and plotted.

Excursion

Popular, light,
uncomplicated, two men
robbed raspberries

from the edge of a ravine
to eat on a bridge—
comma over gorge

(no one
father, not
yet husband)

—driving high,
by atlas,
while I stuck

to complications
& Pavlova,
sugaring the inevitable:

Let yourself
get used to one position
before you move to another.

     **

—an experiment proving nothing except the problem w/ chasing
monuments forever.

The Drink, the Sea

The gypsy winemaker has me
for dinner. He hates expectation
and I am part of the populace,
potare, hand to pet, pretty hair.
My hair smells so good, he needs
to eat it, he says. It's a masque,
I gush, mouth double-happy
with grapes. Man of socks
and scandals, sandy
cracks and women castled,
he thumbs a cork and shows me
pleasure's black hole. Cinaret,
cintarel—who bears varietals?

Think of a name, any name.
Tilt the glass and trace the legs,
he says, hauling out his cellar.
I have not asked so much,
but truth has a greedy nose.
I know I can grow. Rapunzel,
rubescent. I do not thirst for more
than vines, trapping vines, *creeping
plants, including the morning glory,
with showy leaves*. Another tasting:
give me what hurts a lot, an egg
fried on the outside, gold ooze
within. Let me pick.

You and you and you and you.
The process of swallowing, a rush
so contradictious, so now.
Stretch me like the last pour in
a magnum. Splosh me like the first taste.

N is for Nature

Bloom star magnolias
fast first, beneath scalesia
seeds. Trying

not to be sad
—a bust.

—oohkay, Galapagos
repose: angle mirror
below my daisy
while moms glow,
show O-maws,
perineals.

Naturally, I die
by butterfly
needle, lie on my
Love-Me, Love-Me
-Not petals—
kink straws,
suck black parasols.
Eat the orchid
in my ear, baby
boy, if nothing else
nouveauté, nuisette,
novena.

(A natural cycle,
emerge and collapse:
The fish grows to fit his pond.)

Surrender

It's fine to collapse on purpose, to mistake *children* for *sentence*,
when, by guidebook, this little life suddenly seems so empty.

I remembered freedom, sky's mesmeric death, where once I
held my breath a pool's length, too busy to eat, too selfish to
surface, water funky and gross, green, more or less uniform.

Oh, step up, *PLEASE*! Chapters and charts, now I had a deck
of evidence. I said:

"Aren't I sublime?"
"See my pole?"
"Three of hearts?
"My miracle?"

You flickered, I flinched. (Starry starvation, syncope.)
Husband in stairwell under mothy chandelier. (Schnapps,
Darjeeling.) Such safety behind glass: monoammonium
phosphate, sodium and potassium bicarbonate. I tugged the
inspector's tag, down I went, blew his brandied sails, and saw
double-time—gestational, faithless—how an occurrence,
anything to anybody, arrested me.

House Sitter

In one suburb of this longing, a cognac leather sling.
Collapse. Baby's first forgiving table, the legs curved

like French heels. It doesn't hurt to look—go ahead,
I'll hold still. Nothing untoward in this nighttime.

A fine way to cross the street, a perpendicular life
with occasional wincing, platonic sleeps. I should

know nothing will pacify me. About town, Venetian
miles from the ocean, here is a canopy of gauze

and invitations, alms to an eight-legged god, sun, saltair
—bring home a tropical glow with this pygmy palm!

Dear, rats nest in the fronds, the deader the better
for rodents. And with that vegetation, a man stops his drink

and names me the sidewalk Cleopatra. You can want anything
anywhere, the atlas says. Here is Saturday, when I am laid,

quaking hard, light and round in the manner of a bird's breast,
how rosy, how dewsome, here I come, watch me come

—so fast and steady a cunt. Here's Sunday, fenced,
unfenced. *Tu quoque.* How much Frenching

is too much, boy? I get mine. What would you do with
a thick moment off the map? City, town, subdivision,

third-world, fourth quarter, fifth dimensions, cook's
cubby, master suite, rocking horse in the in-law apartment.

Forecast

Others know cave charms, see petals sakura in their laps, no matter the season.

They make a daytrip of it, an adventure, spy a bunnybox beneath the counter, dog's head plates, adidas french flowers, hello mango, hello hello, hey stomach, hi cake, melting halo, paradise pie, *icho* and clover, baby blue shorts that go swish*swish, albums, red boat, interviews.

They like: ultrasounds and sustenance, their mangos stretched ultrasuede: see it, stroke it, touch it, take a profile pic.

Joy, joy, joy! they echo. Nest and pump and latch and love. They love to kick back on vacation. They crave a family getaway.

Show me allure: satori! Where's *my* wristband? How am I blanker than before?

Ullage

One tips nasturtium in the salad. Two calls club moss
lycopodium. Three flips her bottom lip, where hope is
tattooed in Thai. (The more I grow, the more frightening I
become.) Four faints, mint and lemongrass. Five tries hi-fi and
velvet, abusing rosemary, luteous shrubs—doesn't *she* seem
lush? *The extent of biological isolation depends on the ability of
organisms to move and disperse as well as their ability to
withstand terrain that is inhospitable.* Seven clarifies celeriac.
Eight hiccups and headaches. Nine feeds her nursery funds to
the fish. Ten tells time: *just stop.*

Choice

I did not invite the inches
though when you open
a door who knows what

will slip in? Many grains
of nice comprise each
teaspoon, each bowl,

and each bag is only
mouthfuls—a woman
unused to accumulation,

refusal. Do I look like
a mother blaming others?
In this kitchen, craving

attention, all its sticky
nuisance. No, no, no,
I am not here. Confusing

the self with another
is acquiescence—
I'd rather

mango tart. In a cell
with a window plant
and a view of a painted

pony, I remembered
my nobility—disrupting
status quo. Going

against the grain (his
porridge, not mine). Inch,
pound, smaller above,

larger below, classic
iceberg answer, classic
moment on the lips. Closing

the door with my hip.
Kissing the cupboard,
plucking the blinds,

boy, I kill all
my plants. Bury
the flour, burn

the oats: like nothing,
purge all I ate
in the dark.

III

*

There are always two deaths, the real one and the one people know about.
—Jean Rhys, *Wide Sargasso Sea*

Sick Present

The first prescription flopped: unscrew the capsule, powder
the sink, pillbugs dot the drain, histamine, headache, fist.
(Cupel me, cordon me—achoo!) At the machine of making
do, there came applesauce and vanilla custard, pink dish in
the anthological brain.

I pulled knots from my scalp and numerals off clocks, unstuck
every sticker I saw. Geese gathered on grass and grayed the
lawn. Loss calmed me down. Dolled off the dock, boxed my
coughs, brackish in back of the paddleboat. Boscage, balcony,
get-betters (I couldn't).

There were relatives and hamburger buns and treadmills.
Bedroom basement, basement bet: I walked a belt, counted
bricks, combed coleslaw for carrots. And still, medical feels.
Bubblegum, cordial and thrill. In panties, chinoiserie silk,
camisoles.

(Sweetest age of speculation: What could be better than
nothing?)

Tides

Water-land, river-land, eye-land, maldivian, shaka, zori, gneiss.

Wading in waist-high—

wait, where is the waist?   My bulge,

my bilge, my breasts, my rolled

neck: feels like the rest of my life,

totting
weeks to translate days,   number of spanks

to break a piñata,

tucks to snug a sarong;

who is a friend,   who an island-hopper,

the meetings I skip, the meetings I
make,
drugs I drop   in the
courtyard basura.

With my hair still dry. At intake. I could be peaceful or parrot,
calm offshore,

intriguing as an inselberg, at least

give you good drowning—

choke myself cured

with a nut, a net,   how else?

I come from a lost family, screwed
                          below the navel, baby boy.

You only add   a bit to this edition ...

slight rise in sea level

submerging the hilly coast.

Goodness, open this body

rightly disused,
rapid and labored,
ready or not.

The doctor stores
antinomies
in an aqua fridge,

round cornered,
Category X,
safety in the dark

and vain, so vain,
craving feet-up
and a tan

while neighbors
pose pineapples
on the coir.

I need a blouse
that snaps off
at the sternum.

No chance
of being shot
full-bellied,

you baby,
my depraved
grace-note.

The less I deserve
the more merit
in this bounty.

Cabochon

Unbalanced, I wander this large, very damp public garden,
landmark for locals and tourists alike. Balking the bird cage
(when I know only *trying* will save me), there are benches
outside the museum and pools. A man sells shaved ice. I
bypass gazebos, sundials, corncob turnstiles—why, baby boy,
the maternal glue has barely dried!

I pick a gift shop with a fancy paste pot. Elicit a squee: *Back in
the jewel box, You!*

(Glyphs of unicorn, wagging index finger, stern face)

To bow, to break, to hope for pain, to pin and pine all
Sundays. Key-of-heaven, bird of paradise, crozier in this
garden. Plaques have facts: resurrection. Saints soil-blanched:
better, better. Tending it, urging it, nurturing dirt, flowers:
rumpled, petal-barren, silent, sighing, pleasure open as birth,
youth and feminine tribes, of treats tomorrow and better
than I thought, than I held, that I heard, to bower a boy, hence
brigand and boor, save Tuesdays and Saturdays, scythe to
splice the girth ...

(Gurney through the atrium, where graveyard nurses smoke.)

Feathering the Nest

Morning, a loon trumpets
        in alarm; the oriole oranges
his pinnie. Alight in my pen,
        ho hum, I dawn. Look at me,
murky!—alone!—the pity!

        Lacuna of sky and sedge,
frenzy and grass, dynamite sizzle
        inside me, ho hum
explode. I cut, I scythe. I've given up
        complicated life—what more
should I grow? Without margaritas
        and gangings, free of the foxhole,
how do you expect me to come
        when ripples ruche the lake?

When daybreak muddies my face?
        Chanting *fear /fathomable,*
abundance/abuse. The current is
        restless, lashing the dock,
in jest, as a sport: playing
        splish-splash with Ova.

What Am I Doing Here Tonight?

Cruises retain pregnant women and partners in conf. room 8, enticements, education, pavilion level. Quite a collection, says my husband, but who's looking at art? The moms

in long dress, lustrous hair. The elegance of this place (dull lighting). On the table in front of the room, plush placenta, stingray flat. Baby doll and bendy pelvis,

poster of parturient cross-section. Show-and-Tell me: What am I doing here tonight? What new lie do I buy? All the fun fears! Nametag, snack, water to sozzle some joy.

Mom #1 is excited about everything, absolutely everything. #2, the whole thing! Dad #2, diapers and wedding veils; another man: home-life, cooking, playing records, books.

Me? O I alphabetize pain, passenger, patient, power, psyche in a split-second—meet the five Ps, says the nurse. It may seem overwhelming—it is overwhelming!—the first

of many decisions. (What box do I check for unbirth?) Your belly will be swabbed with orange, but then it's over in minutes. The skin is cut, the uterus, baby is out in five.

Sutures: uterus, skin: twenty. Clamps to prevent calf clots. Pale yellow paint to sunny the OR. The catheter, fairy-floss thin. A shot in the back, an IV to swim. Have mumsy

go under? Oh no, no, never! (Why not? Let me go.) Mom #1 believes the surgery will protect baby's brain. Another likes control: Zero risk of tearing. One and done. Pain

is second. Bed rest versus ice packs, scars versus snips, vacuum not forceps, emptiness not gush, the dread or the dread or—de trop—no, the dread, I can't go on here, Boy.

I pray

for more bad days
than good. A little
stunt: malfunction,
mutation, stalled
pink. Hey, chicken
little, to count
your toes, I invert
like angel food.
O I am bored
of such sterile
gravity. I am bored
of white skirts,
peddled on
the Brother,
feeding commands
to the rudders:
Land smoothly.
No jumping!
Cook your fish.
I send for swatches,
shawls, strollers,
strapless bras,
bored of the novel
—I throw it!
One book, one
man, one child,
one house, mind
so orchestral I
yell CELLIST!

Chocolate in
cup, veins
in my breast,
some limpid
emotion, rough
sex, fetch me
mercy to mount,
mercury to gauge,
darkly illiterate starling.
Myelin, I grabbed
(gravid, graceful),
thanks-but-no.
Tongued my own
thumb. Bored in
branches, bored in
snow, bunker-bored,
studio boring, bearing
a husband's tableau.
Boredom so big,
begot Yorkshire
pudding, so boring
this scentless shower,
just bored waiting
on a correspondent
with style. Is it
you, Child? Write
something, south-
paw, amusing.

N is for Nuclear

Beetle big
               as the newborn's nostril
—so quickly, I loved him

against all provocations,   nulliparous

'nother yesterday—no quickening,

no overhead   ,
          no splash

               of   engines and rotors

                              rope choking down

               calm waters.

          I avoid the hostile nest,

     let lover's milk

     soak, pale as bone,
               pale enough

to bubble, to swallow, nuchal enough. If the vessel matters
               —nubuck,

     lug soles, parka

pregnant with pockets.

For station means swap and platter means plate.

I tripled a plan, announced my intention!

But was my wound   honorable?

No.

IV

*

I come out: it is ecstasy.
—Roland Barthes, *A Lover's Discourse*

Let me see it—

silver silo on the prairie—phallus, tower, try—me in the black
sedan unsmoked—half this time, half this womb—one of a
two-horse hitch—the pairing of parent and child—my father
and I—listen to KISS—questions are the age of life—family,
that compulsive anthology—how long have I been voluble,
always the same—attuned to adequation—pizza buffets—my
body is roundly adult—eat it, call me delicious—diet soda the
best way to cancer—all these years, I heard—how motherless
my father—immaculate conception by dad—Tigers and roses
and engineers—a slow boy next door—a freezer stocked with
Hungry Man—a plumber, a housewife, a kidnapping—a
French name hard on the tongue—a small brick house—a
large brick house—a nail through a shoe in a garage—red
barn, white barn, yellow tractor, thin crust, hand-tossed—my
sorry shopping bag wrists—hospital band hidden in bras—
red bulb I bought from Ace Hardware—straight razors spat
like Pez—pricetag ankles—I've been sneaking for years—
slicing slivers of the past—who was she, what am I, one-third
French?—one-third disillusioned—one-third unusable—dial
tone, busy signal, ghost—there was a phone on the wall—my
father tore it off—the cheaper the plate the louder the
break—plastic at Pizza Hut—pepperoni at Pizza Hut—good
salad bar Pizza Hut—halfway between home and school—
learning the castaways in Central Illinois—desolate
downtownery of iron and antiques—Cambridge, Kewanee,
Princeton—a booth—everything blamed on my mother—
bathhouse barns—theater barns—scarping grass—my
mother and the tent and the mud—my mother and the dogs
and the kids—my mother and the money, bam, gone—lady

doctor, lady lawyer, lady engineer—the girls he dated not
her—the lives in Michigan, Iowa—islanded Illinois—ill
Illinois—face greased and mozzarella'd—your sickness is
hard on your mother—I am not embarrassed—she left
them—I do not ask—didn't want him—no mischief in the
past—in the bathroom—abortion or light through a skin—I
used no silverware, retasted the grease—the cows, the cows—
an afternoon—his mother left—I listen—how a man may be
untouched, unwanted, alone, adjusted for no one but a
daughter—retch unto wretch—hearing his heart—this is
why never—never, never—no children—Flying J, Road
Ranger, Love's, Phillips 66—the cows, the cows!—god made
you—god's purpose—to suffer and endure—the sows, the
sows—it's so animal, inhumane—to barf and barf
(background: hairdryer)—it hurt for every woman—she
broke for you, too—what makes you so special—some
delicate flower—how now, brown cow, how now—how now,
young sow—cheese breath—curl head—dry lettuce—cancer
crush—driveway fingerer—harridan—souling the throat—
halfway—searching the countryside—don't ask him—eighty
miles to go, ninety—Lion's Den, adult books—Polynesia in
the cornfields—silk and sequins—do not ask about his
mother—raised by wolves—Spaghetti-Os from the can—
Hershey's syrup misogynist—the myth of Medusaing the
man—minikining the father—living a stay-at-home
sorriness—losing the stocks, losing the logic—getting fat on
the checkbook—paying the bills (Pringles)—eating all day
(General Hospital)—balancing Snackwells and shopping
sprees—he wants to drop dead at his desk—glory days of lab
and ashtray—fun young girls—wet—waterskiing Lake
Geneva—a key to the Wrigley Mansion, a keychain of
handcuffs—Mr. Beef—routine self-abuse or gravy
sandwiches—fluorescence—a daytrip, a flee—the telescope

on a bay in Wisconsin—stars every parent sees—
campouts—a trust fall, a bonfire, a horse—timeless, lucky
and stupid—*one cannot give language—but one can
dedicate*—trails in the rearview mirror—the land as flat as my
backtalk—prairie school, pleasant daughter, pointy nose—
"Strutter," speeding ticket, afterthought—registered, meal-
planned—I am moving out—moving on—into—
trimesters—truck pile-up—semi burn—black car, slow
down—

Coal

My husband has land in a lake, north of the cities, which means I have land, so do you.

> Sears cabin, boat access, outhouse, Darling, coyotes, stumps: not my style island.

From his mother, he has sensibility, toe to tile, standing still, an outlook.

> He sights the high point in every valley and holds his ground. (Thighs, thighs.)

He is fond of red discipline and programs, parks found in the back of the atlas.

> How little he quavers. Since he was a teenager his mother has dreamed of teeth

being pulled from her mouth. Incisors, atonement: alcohol leached from his cells.

> Now, it's his turn: crumble, pulverize, mouthwash, floss, life jacket for infancy.

No season for nervousness, no sand on this shore, twigs and ash and graham crackers.

> Someday, I too will own omens—the onslaught of extraction, a sadness.

I don't know how to handle these pronouns. His son. My property: boy, cake, candle.

Every year our island needs maintenance. Love is a sheath, here's a thicket.

The Viewing Room

Toast and peanut
butter, THC,
maple-syrup
brown glass
species.

with a single
direction—past:
he avails a knee to J,

options R
the grinder.

Lover, vassal,
father,
he spreads
his legs,

drives for fries with MG.

He bodysurfs in Tibet,
in Auckland breaks a rib

and lies in the bed of a pickup

with a girl,
a gun, Godzilla
rolls, brushes

a mustache, sires
five let's-pretend

childs.

And friends
like him
high,

got him
drunk,

Patrón beaches,

stoned lies,
each peripeteia
prefaced—

(Once the baby
is born, how will he
want to?)

He has a scar
on his chin,

is not prone
to hysterics,

but in August
he fights
to drive off

a cliff
and cabinets unlock
for him, amulets
mint, and he hides

desire, a rope
he tugs, he tests
like a bell:

it chimes.

Resurrection

Ascension is off-menu, but abstention—I'll have her biblical nose. Deny every burnt scoop on Ile St. Louis, starve the tourists my chat. See them, so happy to slice lamb, butter bread, buy off children with baskets? Me, I take lunch by the pool, crushed by a bad sun.

All morning, girls hawk huevos, selling plastic shells. Call this Easter lemonade. An anklet makes every calf candy—yes, even yours, little boy. Turquoise cuff, cheerio beads, pearl choker, googly brooch, the loop-de-loo rosary comes to a sequined cross. I can't unsex the crucifix—I won't! Your penis is pacifier, mushroom, plush, O, hush, unblush yourself, we're family now. Palates develop, organs descend, holidays matter little save brunch.

Freedom

Freedom

becomes a man   driving four hundred miles

to lock himself in his cabin

in his pines

on his island

off his lake

to give in

to himself   to his head

while his boys canoe the bowl, the bud ...

**

in the meantime   southwhile

a city called school

teaches me

this is your body off limits.   This is how to curb,
how to cut

        Fridays,
                    alcoholic as lemons in heat.

"Everything Is Calm, and That Is Worse"

With half an orange,
half an apple
six days into vacation—

with tiresome
relaxing, off
your feet,

bondage, dotage,
suspension,
sarcoma, easy

extremes, with
-drawal and wonder,
throat, half-

whipped, half-breasted
—I deserted. Years
or wandering,

mindless ahimsa,
relentless, in stitches,
an islander,

half love,
half death—
I gorge

the volcano,
his whole volcano,
totally unplugged,

fooling my needle,
totally alone
in this cottage

Thalamos

Beyond copse and corpse, hedgerow and scarlet hip,
the tent is white and obvious. Inside, a bride

begins her tour. Her train gone, veil a jubilate
square. Now congratulations and congratulations and

this baby suits you. I have traded my Napoleon
for chicken. I am one sad stop, inevitable as a dandelion

clock. A dessert fork dings the first glass. Cousins
constellate and fib. Look at little mama, how

beautiful, peacocks gawping the photo booth, look
at some smokers off stubbing cigarettes on the empty

lawn. It is easy enough to smile through toasts, friends'
confessions, a brother's snafus in a dress

of Normandy blue. Secrets macramé the neck,
and silence the sonar, starlit in rain.

Across the lawn, our story skips the dogwood grove:
I too walked an aisle, really very happy.

Shower

On eye and ear, the years stream fairly forward,
cardinal and stubborn—another season, the branched
jay watches through the picture window, eyeing death
in the kitchen. A bowl of cream, whipped and souring;
chocolate too black for the honored guest. The table
is toy-clear, but everyone still hears the mobile—

its lullaby moves, slow as molecules mobilizing
a whisper; the animals hang from weak flowers, four
stems, red and blue, yellow, orange, strewn on the table:
here a dolphin and a tiger, there a lion and a branchlet-
legged giraffe, even a corpulent whale. Why must I sour
the song? The wind-up still works, but I like to die.

If I could relive time, would I try my first death,
asleep inside my mother? I was crab-fed and mobbed
by friends, champagne corks shot and smelling of sourdough.
Years of Polish, processed cheese, christened, forewarned:
winter will break everything in sight, ice the branches
off dreaming magnolias. Only booties on the table,

gown knit of bitter purls, a bonnet's strung satin: tableau
called "Joyeux," tissue wads, ghost basements, dearth
of consequences—shiftsplicesplit, baby's branching
breaking my self. Fatigue of ennui, this month's mobility
mock. To the nipple kiss, compression-waist forwardness
of posing with grandmums and aunties, sisters souring

sex for eternity. Yet the chickadees chirp their sorry
crib-song. A wooden pull-along seal toddles on the table.
The favors in tulle: I can use this at home, going forward.
One has to practice softening without softening to death.
I touch the things I touched before, and time immobilizes,
from mother to morning, we gather pussy willow branches

and bouquet the day. On lips and nose, the boy branches
off into tomorrow: sterile bottles, talcum onesies, soured
madness of milk and *I-don't-want-this* mucking the mobile,
barring the beat-up Brahms. No. I can't. I won't be tabled
and tasked, but sly, slightening, slipping off, death-
thin, tippled, charmed. Haven't I calendared forth

for years? The decades branchy and weird, a cabinet of tabletop
cakes and pincers, and Sweetheart, I refuse to be soured.
I flick the mobile and pray for naps, perfect my little deaths.

N is for Northern

The ferry is a fourth term, ocean to archipelago,
days without any visible civilization. No cards,
no dice, only the gamble of latitude—and for me
this is ideal. Don't you like

                the idea of islands? The man asks.

Haven't you islanded your daydreams, detail by detail?
O, but MEN!—I like arbors and arborettes, badlands
and bosques, bowers, caverns, caves and coves; dells
and deltas and dairy farms;

                eddies, estuaries, espaliered

groves; farms and fernland, fecund as fallopia; grotto
upon grotto, gulch and gully; highlands, heights, hills;
kills, lagoons, lowlands, and mountains. The Grand
Mesa. The Bookcase

                Range. Peninsulas and pleasure

domes, quagmires, quarries; canyons called ravines and
ravines called gorges; the forest, the woods, the prairie,
the plain, savannah, tundra, taiga, thrill, evening mining
land's lassitude—

                amorous, stripped. Surely

the island could have my affection, but why? There are no islands,
I plug my eyes. Everything overhead
is horizon: I don't drop by, simply tilt. A bear
approaches her black cub;
                    a raccoon cavils

trackside; I clasp my hands over the hive
and let my palms be stung. Take my pinky
from the socket. No more animals hiding.
No more offspring
                    mangling my will, my mind.

(Island-tan, aphonia shows. Island-bound,
dysthymia glows.) No! Let me train for hours
and make myself cry in this candy box.
Hallucinations, okay,
                    they're mine.

If hunger bothers you, I'll bother myself. I'll walk
through the train, holding onto seatbacks, arrive
at the till. A rum and pineapple or five. Show the man
your purse, silly girl.
                    Here, I say, pour me an island.

V

*

I think you are a special person and ought to live on an island and let the world visit you.
Don't you go visiting the world (you can't have those lines ...)
—Anne Sexton

Everything and fireworks

the night before Mother's Day,
a team of woozy tulips

2 doz/$20,
hours parked

in the driveway,
jigger of vertigo

jiff in the jug,
I am jealous

of you
in the aisle,

aleatory, some
retail clock—

nothing happened
in the grocery storm,

aglow with nerves
and nectar, cards,

carbohydrates:
cast off this

convalescence
and cure my conscience

—paradise
so cumbersome

and worming,
everything overdosed,

overdue. Moonlight
tussive and diamond:

I've learned what I have
to do is a sentence;

what I get to do
is a gift.

N is for N is for N

My soul-sweet, phantom-sweet pilot.

Do you have a poetry yet? A father who remembers Hawaii.
Tennis courts and car seats, mint liquor. Try padre. A mother
who chewed grape garden lilacs. Door County pancakes with
names.

You have no part in adiposity—you must be tired of listening.

Amino

Corn, he tells me
needs its master.
Without

human cultivation
the grain would not
comprise one-third

a complete protein
alongside squash
and beans. Seed

from where, eerie
introduction, who
am I to you? Amid

stalks, sunset
bloods the sky—
yet on I go

eating mousetrap
sandwich. My high
ideals crumb

the quilt; the train
shrills station-ward;
copter

chops foghorn.
Still, I am
willing to take this

starch and altar
it, stain
the areolae,

open my veins
for months,
nurse to scab.

To forge new
crop,
seek a sky

or courage
that forces you
to choke it.

For now,
ritual hips,
stretching

the puss
with lavender
oils and induction.

Kissing Disease

I.

Dawdling one summer, diagnosed with low ambition

(anhedonia of Splenda and cucumbers)

(kitten-heeled flip-flops, polka-dotted dress)

(I have not forgotten the mistakes)
—even now, Lil Mama

II.

(in the suburbs, Reason is an island in the backyard)

(swing, rack, slide, rope)

(sudden country overcome by locomotion)

(never the snuggle-bunny, never the mother's pet)

**

(serious and severed child, totally foul and free)

(proud as an organ)

(ugly as a rabbit)

(bangs, puffed sleeves: don't remember)

(once I misspelled it—rember—red construction paper, age eight)
(still re-member)

Why reproduce these genes?

III.

dawdling season: drama and diet pills, do-it-or-don't aspirina,

                diagnostics, declaratives:

(I'll never have children, kill me if—have you met the woman who raised me?)

(Alice says she'll marry Russian rich, get knocked up, send the brats to boarding school

         —For what? I ask. The furs?

         —The hats.)

IV.

dawdled a man who said you look good in hats

       wear more hats

            (Chewed roadrash at the Speedo showdown,
gummed the gussets on the neon nylon ball cap, once a red bucket
when I was eight: red cowgirl boots, red errors, red jumper, red eyes
from cries or staying up late, steeling myself from my mother)

              **

             boarded coach, a decade of
                haberdashery

              **

       hairnet, sun hat, triplicate, veils

            white paper shower cap in the operating
              room, on the boat!

V.

Let me out—I'm getting out—I'm done

                  dawdling with who I could be

                        drawing women I might become

VI.

I got a train and talked to the marsh,

      counted the islands in Wisconsin,

            turning on the greasy carpet,

           watching the convicts

          —white sneakers, black baggies—

        cup of coffee. Overhead, the stuffed satchel and
          wallets

     of overheard stories, like structure or something

          could save me,

            (grant my prayer)

            like, a sentence I can spell—

VII.

Dawdling the fox swatting my heart, dialing

                              the number pinned to my breast,
                                        beating—

                    I kept myself from the "pure" tragedies,

              hoarding systems and catastrophes

(pink tape, pink gum, pink stain of menstrual almost)

                              misled, maybe, but exciting (!!)

              mailing myself tickets for the future.

**

                              The man I visited gave me a tea set

        with saucers to cover the cups,
                              a sweater, a steak, a ring.

              In the preview, Coca-Cola light: he opened his palm

and placed his wrist on the armrest.

He offered me his pulse, that surgery—
new at my thumb,

twice in my ears, borne.

Notes

The films *Castaway, Chocolat,* and *A Cry in the Dark* inspired early drafts of several of these poems. Language from *Rosemary's Baby* appears in italics on page 8.

Text from Jean Rhys' *Wide Sargasso Sea* appears in italics on page 29.

Text from Roland Barthes' *A Lover's Discourse* appears in italics on pages 1 and 45 and as a title on page 58.

Text from *Anne Sexton: A Life in Letters* appears in italics on page 65.

Definitions and etymologies courtesy of *Webster's New World Dictionary of the American Language* (College Edition, 1964).

Acknowledgments

Thanks to the editors of the magazines in which these poems first appeared:

AGNI: "Shower"
Bayou Magazine: "What Am I Doing Here Tonight?"
Bennington Review: "Coal"
Denver Quarterly: "Let me see it—"
jubilat: "Progress," "Volatiles"
North American Review: "Thalamos"
West Branch: "Trimester"

I owe an immense thanks to the following friends who helped me revise these poems, and this manuscript: Monica Berlin, Alec Hershman, Eileen G'Sell, Kerri Webster, Erin Pienaar, Melissa Carroll, Andrew MacDonald, and Jon Riccio. In addition, Wendy McCredie and Leonard Schulze's generosity in cinema and conversation provided solace and inspiration while this manuscript was composed. To my mother and father, who continually show me the value of living with heart. Finally, I am grateful to Thomas Cook, who is tireless in the courage and rigor he brings to the page.

JoAnna Novak short story collection, *Meaningful Work*, won the 2020 Ronald Suke-nick Innovative Fiction Contest and was published by FC2. She is the author of the novel *I Must Have You* and two books of poetry: *Noirmania* and *Abeyance, North America*. Her work has appeared in *The Paris Review*, the *New York Times*, the *Washington Post*, *The Atlantic*, and other publications. Her essay "My $1000 Anxiety Attack" was anthologized in *About Us: Essays from the Disability Series of The New York Times*. She is a co-founder of the literary journal and chapbook publisher, *Tammy*.